What to Do When It's

NOT FAIR

A Kid's Guide to Handling Envy and Jealousy

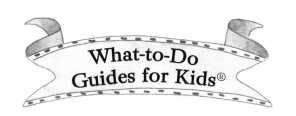

What-to-Do
Guides for Kids®

What to Do When It's

NOT FAIR

A Kid's Guide
to Handling
Envy and Jealousy

by Jacqueline B. Toner, PhD
and Claire A. B. Freeland, PhD

illustrated by David Thompson

MAGINATION PRESS • WASHINGTON, DC
AMERICAN PSYCHOLOGICAL ASSOCIATION

Published by
MAGINATION PRESS
An Educational Publishing Foundation Book
American Psychological Association
750 First Street, NE
Washington, DC 20002

For more information about our books, including a complete catalog, please write to us, call 1-800-374-2721, or visit our website at www.apa.org/pubs/magination.

Printed by Worzalla, Stevens Point, WI
Book design by Sandra Kimbell

Library of Congress Cataloging-in-Publication Data
Toner, Jacqueline B.
What to do when it's not fair : a kid's guide to handling envy and jealousy / by Jacqueline B. Toner, PhD and Claire A.B. Freeland, PhD ; illustrated by David Thompson.
pages cm. — (What-to-do guides for kids)
ISBN-13: 978-1-4338-1341-2 (pbk.)
ISBN-10: 1-4338-1341-6 (pbk.)
1. Jealousy in children—Juvenile literature. 2. Jealousy—Juvenile literature.
3. Envy—Juvenile literature. I. Freeland, Claire A. B.
II. Thompson, David, illustrator. III. Title.
BF723.J4T65 2014
152.4'8—dc23
2013005781

Manufactured in the United States of America
First printing April 2013
10 9 8 7 6 5 4 3 2 1

What-to-Do Guides for Kids®

**What to Do When
Bad Habits Take Hold**
A Kid's Guide to Overcoming
Nail Biting and More

What to Do When It's Not Fair
A Kid's Guide to Handling Envy and Jealousy

What to Do When You Dread Your Bed
A Kid's Guide to Overcoming Problems With Sleep

What to Do When You Grumble Too Much
A Kid's Guide to Overcoming Negativity

What to Do When You Worry Too Much
A Kid's Guide to Overcoming Anxiety

What to Do When Your Brain Gets Stuck
A Kid's Guide to Overcoming OCD

What to Do When Your Temper Flares
A Kid's Guide to Overcoming Problems With Anger

CONTENTS

Introduction to Parents and Caregivers

Envy is part of your emotional repertoire. You may feel envy when you wish you had what someone else has: a bigger house, a better car, a certain vacation. You may become jealous of another person's preferential attention from time to time, such as when your boss favors your co-worker, or your friend is busy with others. And just like you, children confront envy—and its cousin, jealousy—on a regular basis and in many different contexts. However, adults are able to keep in perspective what children haven't learned yet: that desires and envy come and go.

Children who struggle with envy get over-focused on what someone else has that they want. They react inappropriately to the good fortune of others. They crave the attention of parents, teachers, and peers. They feel their own identity is based upon experiences or recognition that others have and that they want. Furthermore, children may not understand or recognize that they are feeling envy, and may act aggressively, have temper outbursts, or exhibit other misbehavior. Alternatively, a child may become withdrawn, giving up on developing a skill or reaching a goal. Envy is a difficult emotion that can interfere with family relationships, affect friendships, and lower self-esteem. If such problems are rooted in envy, what can you, as a parent, do about them?

What to Do When It's Not Fair will teach your child how to gain perspective by identifying the thoughts that produce envy and developing alternative thoughts that may not eliminate envy, but will reduce its impact. When thoughts change, inevitably emotions and behaviors do as well. With practice, children can learn to think more realistically. When they do, they are less likely to be thrown off course by envy.

Parents often feel compelled to respond to the behaviors at hand first. A sulky, uncooperative child might be asked to "take five" and come back with a more cooperative attitude. That will likely result in temporarily improved behavior, but you may need to help your child increase her self-awareness and develop coping strategies for the next time envy rears its ugly head. Children who struggle with envy will need extra help dealing with the feelings and behaviors associated with this emotion.

Directly addressing their fears–of losing your attention (or that of another parent or adult), of wanting what someone else has, of feeling left out, or of feeling inferior—may be helpful.

Also, parents can teach important lessons about expressing gratitude for what one does have, forgiving and forgetting, and being generous with others. You have probably tried reminding your children of their good fortune at other times or in other situations. Perhaps you pointed out items or opportunities that they have that others do not. Or maybe you've reminded them of the fun they've had in the past with friends whom they currently feel have overlooked them. If you have more than one child, you've certainly explained repeatedly that fairness doesn't mean always getting one's way and that, in a family, it's important that everyone has an opportunity to have a turn or to make a choice for all. No one person can always control that TV remote! However, some children have a harder time than others accepting these messages. They need more help recognizing envy and thinking about their experiences differently. Our emotions are not driven merely by what happens to us, but also by how we understand and interpret those events. Parents can gently guide a child to think differently about uncomfortable, unfortunate, or envy-provoking situations. Children can learn to challenge their initial thoughts, and get past their envy.

We hope that this book will aid you in your efforts to help your child learn to cope with envy. We encourage you to read through the book first on your own. A basic understanding of the psychology underlying the techniques in this book will help you to coach your child effectively. Then, begin to read with your child, a chapter or two at a time. As you do so, perhaps you will recall recent events your child faced that mirror those presented. If so, consider reminding your child of those occasions. If he became upset at the time, explore ways in which he might think differently now, benefitting from examples in the book. And by all means, if he coped well with a situation that prompted envy, praise him for his skill. Inquire about what thoughts he used to manage those feelings of envy. By underscoring such successes, you will encourage your child to use the strategies again.

Keep in mind that learning to analyze thoughts is a developmental process. Children of different ages will vary in their ability to come up with alternative thoughts. However, you can coach your child to reflect upon her own thoughts and, perhaps, with practice, think differently. At the very least, noticing thoughts, feelings, and behaviors together will give your family a format for addressing emotional experiences.

Of course, simply reading a book with your child won't instantly result in an ability to cope with envy. That will take plenty of guided practice and experience. The examples and discussions in the book are designed to help you talk to your child productively about ways to challenge envy thoughts. By doing so, you are supporting the development of your child's coping skills. We encourage you to reinforce new learning about the connection between feelings, thoughts, and behaviors regularly. Your child won't be freed from all feelings of envy, but you will hear "it's not fair" a lot less often.

CHAPTER ONE

Yo Ho Ho!

It's fun to pretend to be a pirate.

You go aboard your ship with your mates, sail the mighty seas, and look for treasure.

Your trusty parrot is on your shoulder, the sun is shining, and your treasure map is pointing you to a huge chest of gold coins.

"Yo ho ho," you call out.

What a great life this is!

A fantastic day for a pirate might include:

- A big pirate ship with a crew of strong and courageous shipmates.

- An enormous chest of the finest gold coins.

- A loyal parrot for a pet.

Draw or write about
a great day for a pirate.

What makes you happy?

Lots of kids feel that an especially happy day might include getting special attention, receiving a new toy, winning a game, or going somewhere super cool.

It feels good to win and to have special treats and activities.

Now that you've created a pirate's dream day, imagine one of your own.

What's your idea of a fantastic day?

Draw or write about a great day for you.

Wouldn't it be wonderful to be happy all the time?

But nobody is happy all the time. Sometimes stuff happens that gets in the way of having a happy day, like when a pirate accidentally drops his gold when he's carrying it back to his ship, and it falls to the bottom of the sea. That would certainly mess up a really great pirate day.

Sometimes a great day is ruined not by bad events or bad luck, but by certain feelings that get in the way. One feeling that can get in the way is **ENVY.** Envy is a feeling that happens when someone else has something you think is better than what you have, or does something better than you, or gets more attention than you do.

Here's how it works:

Remember that huge treasure chest of gold? Suppose our happy pirate spies another pirate ship and right there on deck is an even bigger chest of gold than his. Before, the pirate was thinking, "I have a great, huge treasure." Now the pirate may think, "My treasure is not so big after all. I want a bigger treasure." He went from really happy to upset because envy got in the way.

Have you ever felt upset without really knowing why or what to do about it? Have any of these situations happened to you?

- You spend all day putting together a  Halloween pirate costume from items you have around the house. Your friend has a really authentic-looking one his mom bought for him. You **envy** your friend's amazing costume.

- You try out for a trumpet solo, 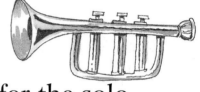 but you aren't picked. You **envy** the kid who was picked for the solo.

- You miss kicking what would have been the winning goal. You **envy** the other team's win.

Envy is the feeling that a person has when they want something that someone else has. Notice that in each situation someone else has something better or wins at something or gets more attention—that is, in each case someone else is involved. You don't feel envy unless you are comparing yourself or what you have or your situation to someone else's. Remember, the pirate with the gold coins was satisfied with his treasure until he saw another pirate with even more treasure. Then he envied the other pirate.

Envy has its good points. If you envy how well someone plays the piano, you might decide to practice more. If you envy a friend's toy, you might help out around the house by taking on extra chores to earn the money to buy one for yourself. If you envy your classmate's math skills, you might work harder in school.

But envy can cause problems. It can put you in a bad mood. And when you're in a bad mood, you might do something that gets you in trouble. Envy can make you frustrated and make you give up trying.

Think about a time you felt so much envy that you got really upset. Maybe your friend came to school with a really neat toy that you wanted. Maybe your sister got to go someplace with your grandma that you wanted to go. Maybe your neighbor's picture was in the newspaper for winning the gymnastics tournament. Maybe a group of kids went to the movies and didn't invite you. Or maybe it was something else that was **NOT FaiR!**

Show or describe how you felt in the box on the opposite page.

Draw or write what made you feel envy.

This book will teach you about causes of envy and how to handle this tough feeling, so you can sail the high seas with pleasure!

CHAPTER TWO

Put Down Your Spyglass

Perhaps you've noticed how in movies and books pirates often use a spyglass. They use it to focus in on other ships or land in the distance.

Of course, while they focus in on small things in the distance, they miss seeing other things around them.

Sometimes they miss big, important things. Sometimes they miss having fun. Sometimes they miss the beautiful treasure they already have!

People in the real world sometimes focus in too closely and miss things too. Have you ever been watching a TV show so closely that you didn't hear your mom call you to dinner?

Sometimes kids become too **FOCUSED IN** when they see something that other kids have that they really wish they had. It can be a thing, like a toy or a really nice yard. It can also be a chance to do something, like taking a trip or learning to sail a boat. When a kid finds out that someone else has something he would like or is doing something he would like to do, he may feel envy.

Just like a pirate using a spyglass, a kid may **FOCUS IN** on that one thing he wants. When that happens, that kid may not notice all the good things he already has.

Sometimes kids can feel envy about other kids, too. Imagine this:

Will just got a new video game. Not just any game, but the one all the kids have been talking about. It is so super cool that everyone—Aaron, Eli, and India—wants to go to Will's house after school to play it. Lela feels pretty full of envy. She finds herself focusing in on the group of kids running off to play the video game that she wishes she has. She wishes the kids were coming to her house. She feels so upset that she goes home instead of joining the other kids at Will's house. She is so envious that she misses joining them and she misses having a turn at playing a cool new game.

That sounds so UN-fun, doesn't it?

Here's another example.

If your best friend gets a really cool basketball, you might focus in your spyglass on that and wish you had one like it. You might miss seeing that you already have:

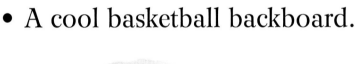

- An awesome basketball jersey.

- A good, old basketball.

- A cool basketball backboard.

- A BEST FRIEND!

The tricky thing about focusing in with a spyglass is that you may see great things that you want, but miss seeing great things you already have. When this happens, your envy can really interfere and make you unhappy. It can make you forget good things you have, it can make you stop doing things you enjoy, and it may even make you get angry at another person. And when people get angry, they sometimes say or do things that hurt others.

If you find yourself feeling envy, you could ask yourself, "Am I being a pirate? Am I focusing in too much on something I want? Am I missing other things that are important?"

So what is a pirate (or kid like you!) to do?

Take control of your spyglass! Don't keep it aimed just at that one thing you want. Look around without it and see if you already have some great things that you forgot to think about. Put down your spyglass so you can see what you do have, and not just things you wish you had. After all, a pirate who keeps his spyglass focused only on a treasure he wants may not think about the gold he already has, or his awesome pirate ship, or his mates!

Emma isn't doing a very good job of putting down her spyglass.

She's so focused on what she wants—
a puppy—that she's missing all the cool pets she already has.

Can you spot what she is missing?

Emma's Cool Pets:

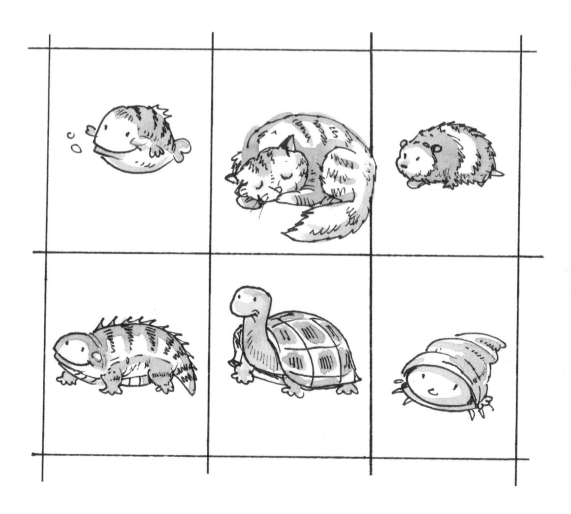

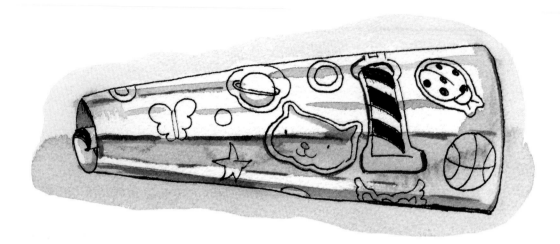

Now it's time to try it yourself. Make your own spyglass and experiment with focusing in on one thing. Then, put it down! See how much you were missing.

Step One: MAKE YOUR OWN SPYGLASS

1. Ask your parents for a cardboard tube, the kind that comes inside a roll of paper towels. Or roll up a piece of construction paper and tape it so it stays rolled up.

2. Decorate your spyglass if you'd like. You can cover it with stickers or construction paper or draw pirate designs on it.

Step Two: Be a Pirate

1. Okay, now stand in a room that has some of your favorite toys.

2. Look around the room at everything. What do you see?

3. Close one eye and look through the spyglass with the other.

4. Focus your spyglass on one toy.

5. Think about other things in the room. What are some toys that you really like that you can't see while you look at that one thing through the spyglass this way?

Step Three:
PUT DOWN YOUR SPYGLASS

Now, look around without your spyglass. What do you see? Do you remember all the things you like? Do you see all the stuff you have? Can you focus on all this?

So, just like when you focused in on one thing with your homemade spyglass, can you think of a time when you might have been so focused in on something you didn't have that you missed good things that you did have? What if you saw a teammate walk onto the field with just the kind of soccer cleats you wanted? Would that make you forget the last new piece of sports equipment you got? What if your friend told you about going to the amusement park and riding the new roller coaster three times? Could that make you forget to think about the fun you had on your own summer vacation?

Draw or write about a time when you focused in on something you wanted so much that you forgot to think about what you already had.

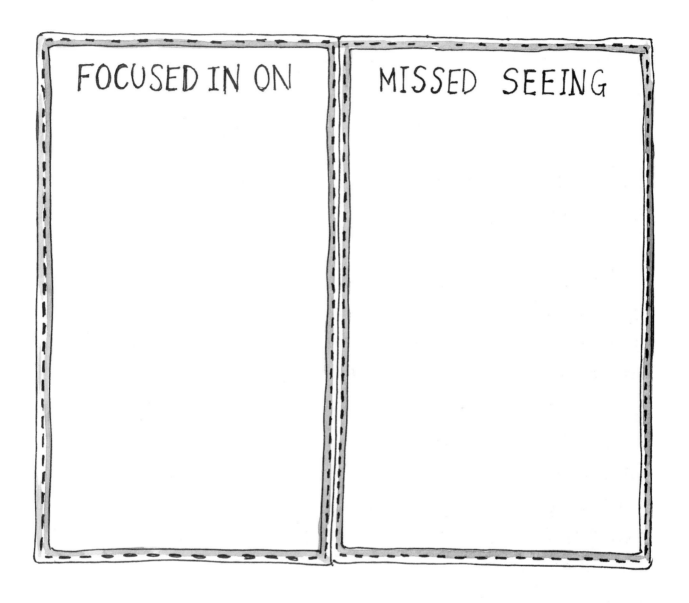

FOCUSED IN ON	MISSED SEEING

If you're having trouble thinking of an example, ask your mom or dad for help. Next time you find yourself missing the good things around you, remind yourself to be a smarter kind of pirate. Envy won't interfere as much if you learn to put down your spyglass!

CHAPTER THREE

Steer Your Ship

A pirate relies on the wind in his sails to power his ship over the sea. But the wind may not always blow in the direction that the pirate wants to sail. In fact, sometimes the wind may blow him into danger. A smart pirate doesn't just let the wind take control of his ship. He checks his map to find the right course, he uses charts of the ocean floor to know where dangerous rocks and shoals lie, then he grabs hold of his steering wheel and follows a safe route to his destination.

Sometimes people can have ideas that lead them in the wrong direction. Just like a smart pirate, they need to look for a different route and steer their thoughts in a direction that avoids problems ahead.

Let's think about real situations where changing the course of a person's thoughts can help them. Do you have a brother or sister? Do they ever get to do things that you don't? Does that ever make you upset? It sure bugs Sofia!

Sometimes people make the mistake of letting their first thought blow them into rough waters. Sofia's first thought is, "Mom likes Carlos best so he gets special TV time **AND** special time to be with Mom." Of course, that seems unfair and makes Sofia feel envious. And when Sofia feels envious, she is grumpy.

But what if Sofia took control of her steering wheel and changed the direction of her thoughts? She might start searching for other reasons why Carlos gets to stay up later than she does.

Which of Sofia's thoughts makes the most sense to you?

Thinking different thoughts may change how Sofia feels about Carlos staying up later than she does.

When she thinks differently, she feels less envy and she goes off to bed feeling less grumpy.

Draw what you think Sofia's face would look like if she believed each of these different reasons why Carlos gets to stay up later.

CARLOS IS OLDER THAN ME.

MOM TOOK ME TO A MOVIE LAST WEEK WITHOUT CARLOS.

CARLOS DOES MORE CHORES THAN I DO.

I GET TO WATCH T.V. WITH MOM WHILE SHE MAKES DINNER AND CARLOS DOES HIS HOMEWORK.

Don't you think it's cool that, when Sofia can map out more realistic reasons for something that's upsetting her, those different thoughts change how she feels?

Guess what? You just learned something new.

WHAT PEOPLE THINK AFFECTS HOW THEY FEEL!

When you search for different ways to think about what's happening to you, those new views may change how you feel!

Let's try another example. Help Michael steer his ship in a better direction and search for a different thought.

Michael's brother gets straight As. Michael thinks: "Jeremy is smart—he's on the honor roll every semester. I'm not smart like Jeremy."

In a family, each person has talents. Michael's brother may study a lot and be talented in schoolwork. But Michael is a skilled artist and has a very creative mind. He can draw fantastic sports cars with lots of details. He even won a prize in the school art show.

When Michael thinks, "My brother is smart; I'm not," he feels envy.

When Michael thinks,

" _____ ,"

he feels better.

Fill in what you think Michael could think instead.

Changing thoughts helps Emma feel better too.

Emma feels envy because her father spends a lot of time with her older sister.

Let's help Emma change her thoughts so she can steer her ship in a better direction.

At different times, parents spend more time with a particular sibling than at other times. Emma's older sister may need extra help with homework or extra cheering up.

When Emma thinks, "I want the same amount of time with my father as my sister gets," she feels envy.

When Emma thinks,

"_____,"

she feels better.

Fill in what you think Emma could think instead.

Not everyone has a brother or sister. That doesn't matter—only children also feel envy at times.

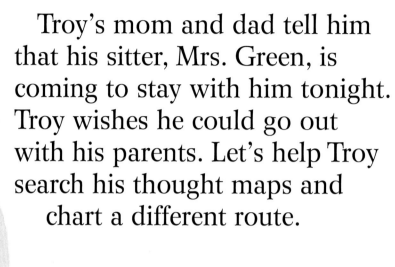

Troy's mom and dad tell him that his sitter, Mrs. Green, is coming to stay with him tonight. Troy wishes he could go out with his parents. Let's help Troy search his thought maps and chart a different route.

Adults need grown-up time sometimes. When parents go out without children, they often go to places that kids would find boring.

When Troy thinks, "No fair! I want to go out with Mom and Dad," he feels envy.

When Troy thinks,

" _____ ,"

he feels better.

Fill in what you think Troy could think instead.

See? When Michael, Emma, and Troy searched for a different thought, they changed their course and they helped themselves feel better.

But sometimes a pirate hits a storm and can't control his ship in the mighty waves. At a time like that, his maps and charts won't help because there may not be a way to avoid the storm. Envy can work that way too. Sometimes there are thoughts and feelings you just have to live with. You may discover some situations that really are…not fair. Then what do you do?

You have to **LET GO** of envy. For example, Isabel's grandmother brings Isabel and her sister shirts. Isabel's is red and her sister's is green. Isabel feels envy because she likes the green one better. But Isabel knows that when you get a gift, you need to say "thank you," no matter how you feel. Not complaining about the color you get is a way of letting the envy go.

When you have a strong feeling like envy, it can seem like you're never going to feel better.

But if you wait, the feeling doesn't last. It's like a wave–it rises and falls.

Eventually, the feeling pretty much goes away. You **LET GO**.

Now you practice.

List three envy thoughts you have—perhaps something you envy about your siblings or something that happened that made you feel envious.

Decide if you should search for a different thought or let your envy thought go:

My envy thought is: **Circle one**

1. _____

_____   Search for a
different thought.

_____   Let go!

2. _____   Search for a
different thought.

_____

_____   Let go!

3. _____   Search for a
different thought.

_____

_____   Let go!

When you put your envy thoughts into words, you can decide how best to chart your course and head in a good direction that works for you.

CHAPTER FOUR

Keep Your Ship Sailing

What if a strong wind suddenly blows a pirate off course? His ship could be blown into a tight cove full of sandbars and boulders. If he can't find a way around them he could get stuck in shallow water or, worse, hit a rock and bash a hole in his ship! Luckily, our pirate is prepared. He's gathered maps of every cove around. He has navigation tools to help him figure out exactly where his ship has drifted. And, most important of all, he's practiced maneuvering his ship in and out of tight places.

When envy blows you toward shallow, rocky waters, you too can be prepared. Envy thoughts can sneak up on you, but just like a pirate who practices dealing with obstacles in his way, you can prepare yourself for those challenging times when you might feel envy—before they happen!

The truth is that there are lots of common experiences that can make someone feel envy. These situations are called envy **TRiGGeRS.**

There are some triggers that will make almost anyone feel envy. Triggers like feeling left out or ignored by your friends. Those things can make you think things that are just not true!

Here's the good news. You can spend a little time when you're not feeling envy to try to figure out what triggers you often have that make you upset. It's kind of a way to make your thinking stronger.

And even better—you can prepare yourself to deal with these situations if they happen. It's impossible to set sail when your ship has run aground!

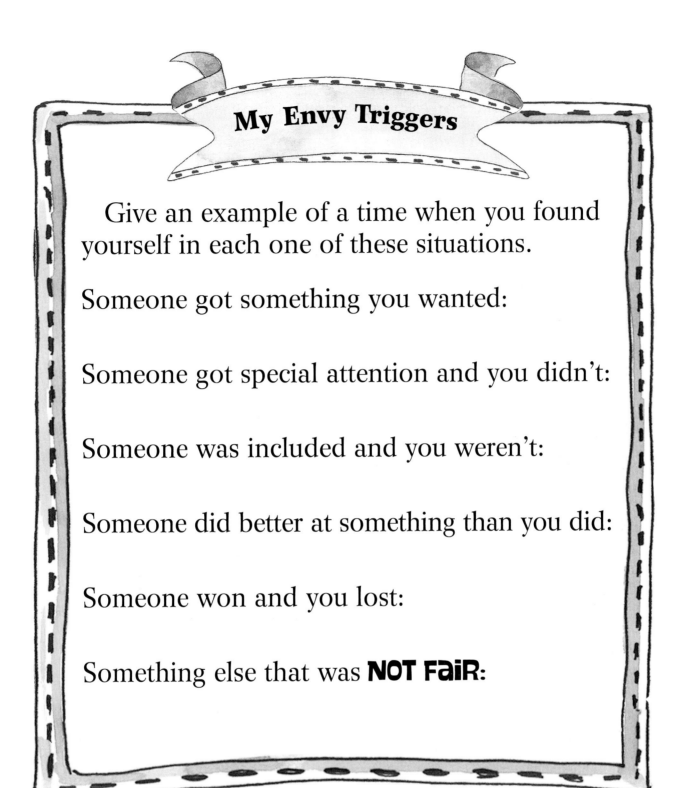

My Envy Triggers

Give an example of a time when you found yourself in each one of these situations.

Someone got something you wanted:

Someone got special attention and you didn't:

Someone was included and you weren't:

Someone did better at something than you did:

Someone won and you lost:

Something else that was **NOT FAIR**:

Go back and put ★★★ by the ones that upset you the most or that happen a lot, ★★ by the ones that upset you a little bit or that happen sometimes, and ★ if it's not a big problem.

Think of your envy triggers as rocks in shallow water. You need to steer carefully around them to get your ship back out to sea. The first step is to identify your envy thoughts that were prompted by envy triggers.

Let's imagine that you drive by your friend Allison's house and see that she has some other kids over to play and she never called you. Everyone is having a great time squirting each other with water blasters and spray bottles. Some kids even have water balloons!

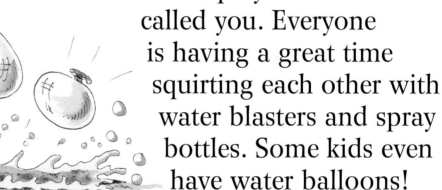

Take a minute and think about what thoughts you might have if this happened. Can you list three envy thoughts that might pop into your head?

1.

2.

3.

The next step is to challenge your envy thoughts and steer through them to calmer waters.

CHALLENGE THOUGHTS can be another way to look at things, or they can tell us that our envy thoughts just don't make sense. If someone was having envy thoughts about feeling left out, they might challenge those thoughts with these:

- I get invited to lots of parties.
- My mom doesn't like me to have a lot of kids over at one time. I'll bet my friend's mom has that same rule.
- If I go out and ride my bike I often find friends outside to hang out with.

Do some of those thoughts seem more realistic than that envy thought that first popped up? Often, when you see things in a more realistic way, those feelings of envy shrink. Now it's your turn. Think of three thoughts that prove that the envy thoughts you might have when you feel left out don't make sense:

1.

2.

3.

How's that? Do these thoughts make more sense? Would they make you less upset?

Now, get two crayons or colored pencils, a red one and a blue one. Red is for hot, upsetting thoughts. Use it to circle **ENVY THOUGHTS**. Blue is for cool, calm thinking. Use blue to circle **CHALLENGE THOUGHTS**.

You're getting good at steering your ship away from envy! You've learned to put down your spyglass so you don't miss something important, and you've seen that changing your thoughts helps you feel differently. You've even practiced letting go of some of your envy by riding the wave. With all that you're learning, you'll be a really smart pirate and keep your ship sailing.

CHAPTER FIVE

Pull Up That Anchor

Have you ever had a friend who kept beating you at a game? Did you feel really bad and kind of angry? If so, maybe you had some of these envy thoughts (even if you didn't realize it at the time):

- We **always** play games he's good at.

- He has **all** the luck.

- I **never** win.

Take another look at these envy thoughts. Do you notice that each one is hopeless and forever? Thoughts like those might make a kid want to stop playing a game.

When you think like that, it's like you've dropped a heavy anchor—your ship can't sail at all. Ever.

You've got to pull up that anchor. Here's one way to help you think differently. Ask yourself:

Is what happened going to last **FOREVER** or is it something that will last just **FOR NOW?**

At first it may seem like you're stuck in a losing situation that will last forever. If you were, your envy would make you feel really bad!

You might feel so bad that you want to stop playing with your friend and not get together with him for a long time.

Wow! That's pretty stuck!

Haul up that anchor of envy by thinking of a **FOR NOW THOUGHT.**

Let's try it. Is your friend going to win every game, forever and ever? Or do you think he might not win next time, or the time after that? Is it possible that you might practice or play better and win next time? Or play a different game and win?

When your friend is winning repeatedly, it can seem like it will go on forever, when actually, if you think about it, that could change. More importantly, you aren't going to be playing this game with him forever.

So think of some for now thoughts instead:

- I guess he's really into this game today, but yesterday he played what I wanted to play.
- He feels happy about how well he can play this game.
- If we keep playing, the practice will help me get good at it too.

Those **FOR NOW** thoughts probably won't make you feel really happy. Maybe you'll end up feeling bored or impatient. But that's better than if you thought you'd never have fun with your friend ever again.

Have you ever felt envy when your parents decided that your family will go to a restaurant that they like and you don't? No fair! You want to pick the restaurant! Or maybe your friends chose to play a game that another kid suggested instead of the really fun thing you'd been looking forward to playing with the group.

What kind of **FOREVER** thoughts might go through your head at times like these?

- "My parents will never let me pick my favorite restaurant."
- "My friends never choose what I want to do."

How might you use **FOR NOW** thoughts to fight those **FOREVER** thoughts?

- "Maybe I can choose the restaurant next time."
- "These friends don't really like tag. I can ask some other friends to play tag."

Do the for now thoughts seem more realistic?

Remember, ask yourself: *Is what happened going to last* **FOREVER** *or is it something that might be just* **FOR NOW?**

Think about a pirate who sails from island to island to look for treasure. He needs to pull up his anchor and get going. If he can't pull up his anchor, he won't get to the treasure. **FOREVER** thoughts keep you stuck. Use **FOR NOW** thoughts

For Now Thoughts

to pull up your anchor and get where you want to go. The more you practice them, the more you'll use them when envy triggers occur. Here are some more examples:

Forever Thoughts

FOR NOW thoughts are not the same as thinking everything will always work out for you. You may still have to wait your turn, accept that you can't have your way, or recognize that you can't always be the best at something. Still, these thoughts usually make you feel at least a little better. **FOREVER** thoughts usually make you feel upset, hopeless, and stuck. So give it a try! Draw expressions on these kids' faces to show how their thoughts make them feel. Do you think their faces would change when they change their thoughts?

In the next week, ask your parents to help you notice when your envy causes **FOREVER** thoughts. Write them down. When you have time to sit back and think, try to come up with a **FOR NOW** thought to fit each trigger. Put a check mark in the "Anchor Up?" column if the **FOR NOW** thought helps you feel better.

Envy Trigger   **Forever Thought**

1. _____   _____

_____   _____

_____   _____

2. _____   _____

_____   _____

_____   _____

3. _____   _____

_____   _____

_____   _____

For Now Thought	**Anchor Up?**
_____	
_____	
_____	_____
_____	
_____	
_____	_____
_____	
_____	
_____	_____

Good job! You'll get to that treasure when you pull up your anchor!

Lighten Your Load

On a pirate ship, the pirate captain is the boss. He decides where to sail the ship and who needs to do what jobs on board. If the pirate captain asks the first mate to plot a course to Dead Man's Reef, the second mate might feel envy. His first thought might be, "Why does the first mate get to study the maps EVERY TIME?"

Kids often have envy thoughts in school. Sometimes when one kid has special attention from the teacher, a lot of the other kids can have envy thoughts pop into their heads.

Look at this picture. This kid is having an "every time" kind of thought. His thought makes him super envious of Joe. If he was thinking that this was happening "this time" he might not have such a strong envy feeling.

EVERY TIME thoughts are like a heavy load slowing your ship down. You can lighten your load by changing your **EVERY TIME** thoughts to **THIS TIME** thoughts.

60

Here's another example: Jasmine's classroom is going to have a special visitor. It's a famous book author who lives nearby. Everyone is excited to meet her. Mrs. Jones tells the class that she'll need a student to show the guest around the school and to sit with the author at lunchtime. Mrs. Jones says, "Jasmine, I'd like you to be the host for our guest."

Well, you know what happens next! **EVERY TIME THOUGHTS** start popping into the heads of some of the other kids!

Did you notice these kids used words like "always" and "every time"? These words can be clues that they think that what's happening is not just happening now but happens all of the time.

Let's help the kids change those **EVERY TIME THOUGHTS** that have popped into their heads and give them some **THIS TIME THOUGHTS** to try. There are two examples in this picture. Can you think of others?

I WISH SHE PICKED ME BUT I DID GET TO READ THE ANNOUNCEMENTS LAST WEEK.

THIS WILL BE GREAT FUN. I CAN'T WAIT TO MEET MY FAVORITE AUTHOR IN PERSON.

THE COMPLETE BOOK OF PIRATES

Let's try another example. Maria is mad because her coach hasn't put her in the game today.

Help Maria change her **EVERY TIME** thought into a **THIS TIME** thought. What could she say to herself in this situation?

So, the next time an envy thought gets you upset, ask yourself if you are weighing down your ship with an **EVERY TIME** thought about something that is really just for **THIS TIME**.

When you lighten your load, you'll speed ahead!

When Other People Envy You

One-eyed Pete is an awesome pirate! He has a great ship and tons of treasure, but pirates want to have friends too. One-eyed Pete knows that if Peg-leg Max feels envy he won't want to be friends, so Pete wants to help Max feel good. He knows not to brag about how much bigger and faster his ship is than Max's or that his treasure chest is full. He doesn't show off when Max is around.

Now that you have lots of skills for handling envy, it's important that you have some skills for when others envy you.

What if you're the one with the cool new gadget and your friend is envious?

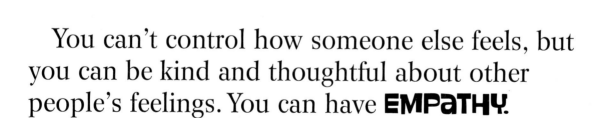

What if you win the game?

What if your dad takes you fishing and your brother and sister don't get to go?

You can't control how someone else feels, but you can be kind and thoughtful about other people's feelings. You can have **EMPATHY.**

EMPATHY means understanding how someone else might feel in a situation. Here are some examples:

Situation	Feeling
Your next-door neighbor is a grandma and her grandchildren live far away.	She probably feels lonely.
Your cousin is going to his favorite amusement park.	He probably feels excited.
A young child is crying as he leaves a Halloween haunted hayride.	He probably feels scared.
Your sister accidentally lets go of her balloon and it floats away.	She probably feels sad.

When you show others that you understand their bad feelings, it can help them to feel better. And, when you understand their feelings, you'll be less likely to do things that might trigger their envy thoughts.

Unscramble these words to figure out how these kids feel.

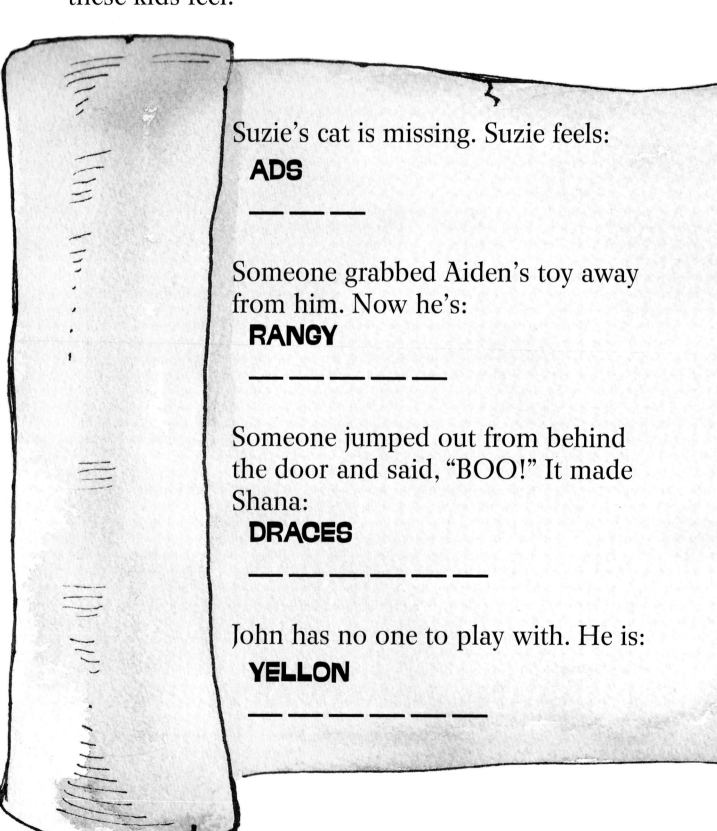

Suzie's cat is missing. Suzie feels:

ADS

— — —

Someone grabbed Aiden's toy away from him. Now he's:

RANGY

— — — — —

Someone jumped out from behind the door and said, "BOO!" It made Shana:

DRACES

— — — — — —

John has no one to play with. He is:

YELLON

— — — — — —

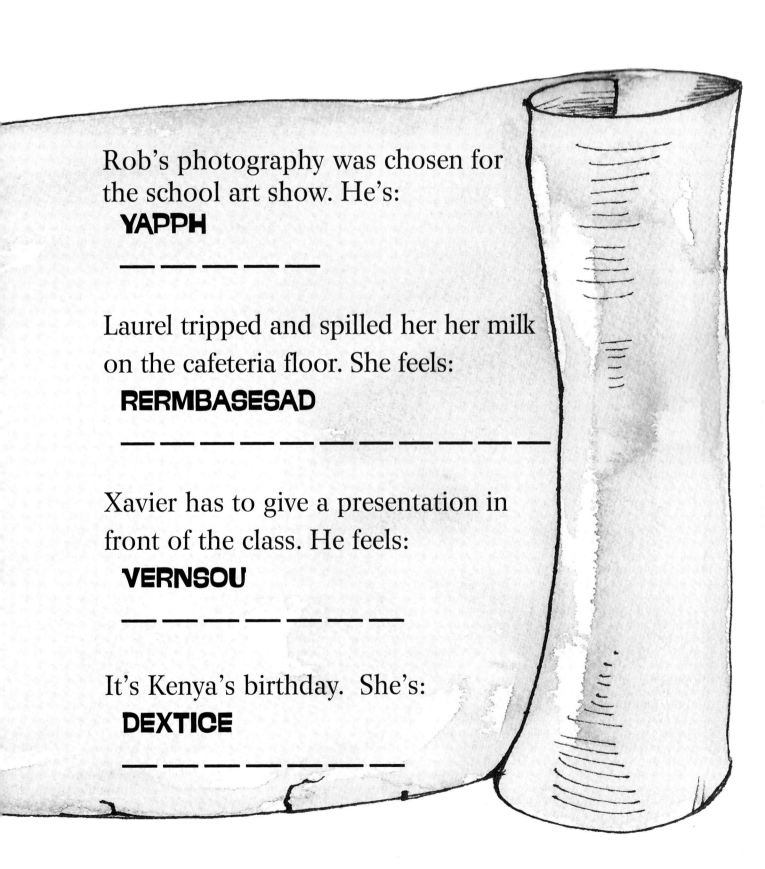

Rob's photography was chosen for the school art show. He's:

YAPPH

_ _ _ _ _

Laurel tripped and spilled her her milk on the cafeteria floor. She feels:

RERMBASESAD

_ _ _ _ _ _ _ _ _ _ _

Xavier has to give a presentation in front of the class. He feels:

VERNSOU

_ _ _ _ _ _ _

It's Kenya's birthday. She's:

DEXTICE

_ _ _ _ _ _ _

You can often guess what people might be feeling by the expressions on their faces, by what they say, and by what you know about the world around you. Then you can speak and act in a helpful way.

Let's look at some examples of times when someone else might envy you. What can you say? Circle the reply that shows **EMPATHY.**

1. Your teacher picked you for the main role in your school play. Your classmate Sarah also wanted the part.

"I got the part because you won't be able to memorize the lines."

"I think you are a great actress. Will you help me practice my lines?"

2. You just won a close tennis match against your friend.

"Good game. You played really well. Let's have a rematch sometime."

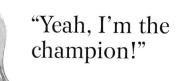

"Yeah, I'm the champion!"

3. Your sister has to miss her favorite TV show, but you get to watch it.

"Ha ha, you're going to miss the show!"

"I'm sorry you have to miss the show."

What can you say in these situations when someone envies you? Fill in the space provided. Hint: Remember the kinds of thoughts that help to fight your envy thoughts. Imagine the other person's **ENVY THOUGHT,** then come up with a **CHALLENGE THOUGHT** that might help them feel better.

You got a B on your test. Your friend, who is also a good student, got a C.

_____

_____

You have a new computer tablet. Your friend shares the family computer at home.

_____

_____

You got invited to a party and your friend was excluded.

_____

_____

Your team won the soccer match by one point in overtime. Your friend was the other team's goalie.

_____

_____

It's okay to feel good when you've received a special privilege or won a game or gotten something new. But be careful when you express your excitement not to hurt other people's feelings. There's a time and a place to shout **"HURRAY!"**

Keep Your Balance

How you feel about yourself can be like standing on a wobbly board—you mostly stay on your feet, but here and there you get thrown off balance and you have to get back up on your feet to keep on going.

People who feel good about themselves keep their balance in life.

74

When you feel good about yourself, envy won't interfere as much. Feeling good about yourself is more complicated than it seems. It doesn't mean that you're perfect, or that you're good at everything you try, or that you're stuck up. It means that you respect yourself, you can handle your feelings, and you feel you're a good person.

People who don't feel good about themselves seem to have trouble staying on their feet. Strong feelings, like envy, can cause them to get too angry or too sad. Then, they might act in ways that get them in trouble.

All About You

Answer the following questions.

1. What is your favorite game? _____

2. What was the last really good decision that you made? _____

3. When is the last time you laughed at yourself?

_____

4. What do you like best about school?

_____

5. The last time someone gave you a compliment, what was it for?

_____

6. What was the last compliment you gave another person? _____

7. What's your favorite color? _____

8. Name a friend. What do you like best about him or her? _____

9. What would your friend say about you?

_____

10. What was the last really hard thing you tried and you didn't give up?_____

11. What's your favorite meal? _____

12. What might you want to be when you grow up?_____

13. How have you stood up for yourself?

_____

14. How have you helped someone else?

_____

Read over your answers. Doesn't being you sound great? If you want to, you can ask your parents the same questions. It might be fun to hear even more things about yourself!

Remember, feeling good about yourself isn't about being the best; it isn't about what you own or winning or getting all As; it's about who you are as a person. It's about being you and doing things that make you proud.

Here's another game to try.

Your whole family will like the "Proud of" game. It works well at the dinner table. The first time you play, have a parent begin by turning to the

person on their right and telling them something they noticed that pleased them, impressed them, surprised them in a positive way, or showed that they learned something new.

Continue this process around the table. Repeat in the other direction.

When you feel good about yourself, a shaky board won't topple you. Hold your head up and **Be You!**

CHAPTER NINE

Take Care of Yourself

Pirates face all kinds of difficulties that can be frustrating and upsetting. Sometimes they handle them easily but sometimes a strong wind or a big wave can interfere with their search for treasure.

Even kids who feel good about themselves get blown off course by envy from time to time.

When people have strong feelings, they can feel them in their bodies as stress.

Here are some ways that people experience stress:

- Feeling wound up

- Not being able to catch your breath

- Having a stomach ache

- Feeling shaky or dizzy

- Having trouble sleeping

- Blushing or getting sweaty

When you are stressed, you can't think as clearly—and if you are going to fight your envy thoughts, you have to think clearly.

You can think clearly and handle difficult situations by learning to relax. With practice, you can get less worked up when something bothers you.

There are lots of ways to relax and they are all helpful. Make a list of what you like to do to relax:

1.

2.

3.

4.

Did you put any of these on your list?
- Listen to music
- Play a game
- Chat with a friend
- Read a book
- Draw a picture

There are many ways to take care of yourself so you can handle envy. Doing something relaxing, getting plenty of sleep, eating healthy foods, and exercising are all important because they keep your body and mind feeling good.

In addition to everyday ways of taking care of yourself, you can learn to slow down your reaction to stress with yoga.

Yoga is a kind of exercise that combines calm breathing with stretching and a quiet mind. If you practice yoga a few times a week, your body learns to respond to upsets in a more peaceful way. When you feel envy, you may not get as wound up. Then you'll be able to remember your challenge thoughts and other strategies.

The following pages will show you some yoga exercises you can try--calm breathing, stretching, and quiet mind. Try practicing them a few times a week.

You will find it easier to handle strong emotions when you've practiced relaxation. Then, when you feel envy, it won't bother you as much and you'll feel stronger, more in control of yourself, and better able to fight your envy thoughts.

Try some yoga and see if it helps you to stay calm.

Calm Breathing

First, lie on your back with your knees bent.

IN 2..3..4...

OUT 2..3..4...

Put your hands on your belly. Notice your breath moving in and out. Do you feel your belly rise and fall? Now try to breathe slowly—in, 2, 3, 4...out, 2, 3, 4.

If your mind starts to wander, just go back to noticing your breathing.

Feel your belly get big and round as you breathe in and gently flatten as you breathe out.

Try breathing in and out 5 to 10 times. Ahhh, doesn't that feel nice?

Stretching

Here are a few yoga poses for you to try. Concentrate on stretching. Only do what feels comfortable.

CAT-COW

Get on hands and knees.

Make yourself into a stretching cat by raising your back up as high as you can.

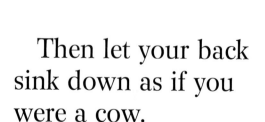

Then let your back sink down as if you were a cow.

Alternate cat-cow about 5 times.

MOUNTAIN/RAISED ARMS

Stand with your feet together and your arms down by your side. Stand as tall and straight as a mountain.

Bring your arms up overhead and reach for the ceiling.

Move your arms back down and stand straight and still like a mountain. Repeat 5 times.

TREE

Begin standing straight
and tall like the mountain.
Look straight ahead.

Lift your right
leg by bending
your knee and place the bottom of
your foot on your left leg. Imagine
roots growing from your left foot
into the ground.
Keep your left
leg strong like the
trunk of a tree.

Stretch your arms up
like branches. If you start
to fall, just try again.
Switch sides.

AIRPLANE

Stand up straight and tall.

Reach your arms
out to the sides.

Tip forward as you
point one foot behind
you. Try to keep your
head and body in line
with your lifted foot.

Keep reaching your arms out to the side.

Switch legs.

COBRA

Come back down to the floor and lie on your tummy.

Stretch your legs out behind you.
Keep your legs and feet together.

With your hands on the floor under your shoulders, lift your head and chest up.

Pretend you're a snake. You can even hiss!

Lie back down and rest and then try it again. Repeat 3 times.

Quiet Mind

Lie on your back with your feet resting open, your arms down by your sides, and your hands face up.

Close your eyes and rest.

Take slow, deep breaths.

Feel your body start to relax.

Stay in this position for 10-15 minutes, or longer if you have time.

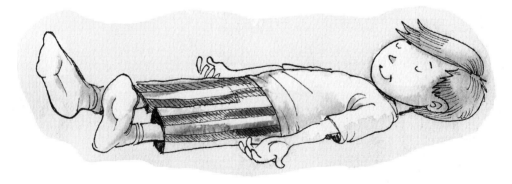

When you practice relaxation, you'll be better able to handle stress. You'll be more prepared to manage your feelings so that envy won't stand in your way.

You Can Do It!

Instead of being a miserable pirate, stuck and weighed down with a **NOT FAIR** anchor, you can sail along more easily by putting down your spyglass to see near and far, riding the waves of upsets, and mastering a new way of thinking.

Envy is a feeling that affects everyone of every age, but you you can prevent envy from interfering with your life—so you get along better and feel better.

Now you know how to handle envy. You can identify **TRIGGERS** and **ENVY THOUGHTS** and you can create **CHALLENGE THOUGHTS** that make more sense. The exercises in this book aren't easy, but if you keep working at them, you'll find that they help you better manage your feelings of envy when they occur.

There will be times when someone else wins, has something you want, gets more attention, or is better at something, but you can handle it. Envy doesn't have to be a problem.

Remember:

Widen your focus.

Challenge your envy thoughts.

Ask yourself if this happens every time or just this time.

Avoid "forever" thoughts.

Let go of envy when you can.

Feel good about yourself.

Take good care of yourself.

There goes envy!

A PIRATE'S SONG

I wasn't invited,
I wasn't picked,
everything feels no fair.

I wasn't the best,
I wanted the toy—
nobody seemed to care.

I cried, I fussed
and I stomped away—
my envy grew so fast.

But then I read this book,
and ahoy!
I put all that in the past.

I put down my spyglass
and changed my thoughts,
stayed with the here and now.

Although it's not easy,
I'm sailing along,
ready to take my bow.

Congratulations. Put your name on this ship and cruise on.